the **manager** as **coach** and **mentor**

ERIC PARSLOE

Second e<

D1458704

Eric Parsloe is the director of the Oxford School of Coaching and Mentoring and the author of several books on maximising individual potential and performance. In the 1970s he founded the Epic Group, an employee communication and multimedia company (now the largest multimedia learning production company in the UK). He was a founder and then chairman of the multimedia industry body BIMA. A former international debater, he has been a selector of the British debate team since 1973, and until recently he was chairman of the Centre for International Debate and Communication Training at the English Speaking Union. He is also a qualified rugby coach.

165 843

Management Shapers is a comprehensive series covering all the crucial management skill areas. Each book includes the key issues, helpful starting points and practical advice in a concise and lively style. Together, they form an accessible library reflecting current best practice – ideal for study or quick reference.

The Institute of Personnel and Development is the leading publisher of books and reports for personnel and training professionals, students, and all those concerned with the effective management and development of people at work. For full details of all our titles please contact the Publishing Department:

tel. 020-8263 3387
fax 020-8263 3850
e-mail publish@ipd.co.uk

The catalogue of all IPD titles can be viewed on the IPD website:
www.ipd.co.uk

the manager as coach and mentor

ERIC PARSLOE

Second edition

INSTITUTE OF PERSONNEL AND DEVELOPMENT

Design by Curve
Typesetting by Paperweight
Printed in Great Britain by
The Guernsey Press, Channel Islands

British Library Cataloguing in Publication Data
A catalogue record for this book is available from the
British Library

ISBN
0-85292-803-3

**INSTITUTE OF PERSONNEL
AND DEVELOPMENT**

IPD House, Camp Road, London SW19 4UX
Tel.: 020 8971 9000   Fax: 020 8263 3333
Registered office as above. Registered Charity No. 1038333.
A company limited by guarantee. Registered in England No. 2931892.

contents

Other titles in the series:

introduction: why coaching and mentoring?

Let's start by agreeing that there is not much that is truly new or original. But sometimes old words and ideas reappear and take on a new significance in a modern setting. That is the case with coaching and mentoring.

In the 1600s 'to coach' meant to transport a valuable person from one place to another. Today we are all encouraged to see ourselves as valuable people who need to constantly transport ourselves from one level of knowledge and skills to another. The 'manager coach' helps this to happen.

Similarly, Greek mythology from more than 2,000 years ago tells us that it was the goddess Athene who took on the form of an Ithacan nobleman called Mentor to act as a friend and guide to Telemachus, the son of Odysseus, during the years of his father's travels. Today the 'manager mentor' acts as the trusted friend and supporter of an individual on his or her modern learning journey in the world of work.

When I decided in 1990 to research and write about coaching and mentoring, I first went to spend a whole day in the library of the best business college in Oxford – Templeton College. I asked the librarian to bring me all the books with coaching and mentoring in their titles. After 20 minutes she returned with a single volume: *Coaching*, by Edwin Singer! Today she would have so many options that she would need a large trolley to carry the books, magazines and learned articles on the subject. Indeed, one visit to the Internet would produce at least 20,000 references alone to 'mentoring in the UK'.

Why this explosion of interest?

There are probably three key explanations:

- First, the rapid – and increasing pace of – change in the way that organisations operate has meant that managers have had to find new ways of getting results. Reliance on traditional hierarchical authority structures no longer works. Coaching and mentoring has provided a practical alternative; a recent IPD survey of 800 UK training managers revealed that 87 per cent of establishments now use coaching and mentoring.

- Second, the cost-effectiveness of the traditional 'training course classroom' method of learning new knowledge and skills has, at long last, been recognised as inappropriate. Coaching and mentoring individuals at their workplace is far simpler, more effective and much cheaper, and provides the essential support to make electronic learning really effective. The IPD survey already mentioned also reported that more than 50 per cent of training managers found coaching and mentoring more effective than traditional training courses.

▲ Third, as the pressure on people to take more responsibility for their learning increases, coaching and mentoring allows organisations to continue to give practical help and support. They can thus retain some influence over their people's development, loyalty and motivation.

So who is this book aimed at and what is it about?

The term 'manager' has a broad definition in the workplace. Some people have it in their job description and title. Others are called 'supervisors', 'team leaders' or 'project co-ordinators'. Some simply aspire to be managers or are specialists who have authority because of their expertise but do not directly manage anyone. This book is aimed at them all.

But the focus of the book is also quite narrow. The aim is coaching and mentoring in the workplace. This deliberately avoids other less robust environments, such as the highly specialised and complex situations of working with the disadvantaged and the disabled or with dysfunctional children and adults, for instance.

There are no absolutes in this field, but the ideas and models I describe are, I believe, generic. However, in the world of modern coaching and mentoring *the context absolutely defines what needs to happen.* The context also determines whether the activity is labelled coaching or mentoring. In practice I do not believe the precision of the label matters one jot.

What matters is that the people involved understand what is happening in their own situation. In most situations what happens is usually a combination of both theoretical coaching and mentoring models. I have chosen to treat coaching and mentoring separately, knowing that people will draw on the theory to create their own contextual models to work with.

My earlier books on this subject were based partly on researching other people's experiences and partly on the lessons I learned from attempting to train people to become coaches and mentors. These influences still apply. But increasingly I have spent more and more time actually being a coach and mentor. As director of the Oxford School of Coaching and Mentoring I currently work face to face with more than 30 individuals each month. So this book is about sharing the experience of 10 years of learning and practical application.

I have tried to balance theory with practicality and simplicity. I have structured my ideas into six chapters:

- *Coaching: the ideal model* of definitions, process, style and techniques

- *Mentoring: similar but different* roles, responsibilities and relationships

- *The essential skills and attributes* that good coaches and mentors require

- *Success lies in simplicity*, with six practical rules to follow

- *Developing the standards* in professional bodies, academia and business

- *Other sources* of information and learning.

Finally, let me explain the terminology I use (and I am not talking about political correctness). An issue of never-ending debate is 'What do you call the people receiving the coaching and mentoring?' This has to be a matter of taste. Some choose the terms 'coachee', 'mentee' or even 'mentoree', all of which I find awkward and rather embarrassing. I have tried 'protégé', 'colleague' or 'partner', only to find that each has particular, and often unacceptable, connotations for some people. So I choose now to use the term 'learner'.

It is my belief that the modern world of work requires everyone to be constantly learning to apply new information, knowledge and skills. In that sense we are all 'learners', and we could sensibly choose to describe ourselves as such. But I would go further. I believe that coaching and mentoring are only means to an end. So I define the overall purpose of coaching and mentoring as:

to help and support people to manage their own learning in order to maximise their potential, develop their skills, improve their performance and become the person they want to be.

1 coaching: the ideal model

I have defined the overall purpose of workplace coaching. But it takes place in a wide variety of situations, from coaching new starters in the skills required in call-centres to helping the managing director to establish the strategic objectives for the organisation. In between these extremes there is a multitude of problem-solving and personal development situations where coaching occurs.

Coaching is a dynamic and expanding workplace activity. But for our purposes it is necessary to try to establish the ideas and theories of an ideal coaching model, while recognising that every coach is likely to behave in the way that seems appropriate to his or her particular situation. Describing an ideal model is therefore not to say 'This is the only way to coach' but rather 'This is a benchmark to make comparison with.' It is also worth reminding ourselves that it is very rare indeed that people achieve 100 per cent perfection. But that does not mean we should not try!

It is probably true that each definition proposed by such writers as Tim Gallwey, John Whitmore or Myles Downey can be said to describe accurately what happens in practice in many day-to-day situations in the year 2000. Organisations have been moving at different speeds towards more sophisticated and effective implementation of coaching. The most important point, however, is that everyone in an organisation should know the definition that applies in their particular situation.

The definition I have become most comfortable with is this:

Coaching is a process that enables learning and development to occur and thus performance to improve. To be a successful coach requires a knowledge and understanding of the process as well as the variety of styles, skills and techniques that are appropriate to the context in which the coaching takes place.

This chapter is about the ideas and theory of coaching, so I will elaborate on this definition.

Coaching as a process

Like all processes, coaching requires each stage to be properly completed if the whole process is to work successfully. Missing out stages or concentrating on just one stage at the expense of the others can lead to confusion and poor results. The coaching process can be illustrated simply in the diagram below; each stage is described in detail in the following paragraphs.

Stage 1: analysing for awareness

Coaching can start only when the learner develops an awareness of the need to improve performance through learning. The manager-coach has to help the learner develop

Coaching process model

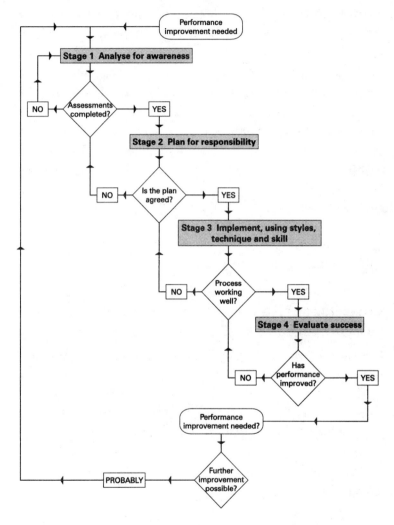

this awareness because, in the same way that you can take a horse to water but cannot make it drink, you cannot coach people until they actually want to be coached.

Learners develop awareness best by analysing their current performance and comparing it with the level they would like to move towards. Having clear standards, or performance competences, to aim for is very helpful, particularly when the coaching aims to develop a specific skill. Using self-assessment as a basis for a subsequent discussion with the coach is a powerful technique for developing awareness.

Stage 2: planning for responsibility

It has long been argued that effective learning and development really occurs only when the individual takes personal responsibility for the outcome. The planning stage of the coaching process is the opportunity for the learner to begin to exercise responsibility.

Coaches cannot, and should not attempt to, impose learning programmes. Learners must be actively involved in the decision-making. Some compromises between an ideal programme and what can realistically be afforded will often be necessary, but experience suggests that trying to agree a personal development plan (PDP) of some kind with your manager is very important.

A successful PDP should answer these key questions:

- What is to be achieved?
- How will it be done?
- Where will it be done?
- When will it start and end?
- Who will be involved?
- Who needs to agree the plan?

In many organisations, individuals are already encouraged to have PDPs. In a minority of instances the PDPs cover any topic that interests the learners. But few organisations are likely to follow this enlightened approach, and most will probably insist that PDPs are clearly linked to business objectives as well as individual aspirations.

To be most effective, a coaching PDP (unlike the traditional annual-appraisal PDP) should focus on only two or three specific development goals over a relatively short time – perhaps only the next three months. It should be reviewed on at least a monthly basis and thus become an integral part of the performance management process.

Stage 3: implementing

Many people regularly experience coaching in the workplace and have done so for years. Unfortunately, although well meaning, it is often *ad hoc*, haphazard and short-lived. In an organisation that wants to take learning seriously this approach is not acceptable.

Coaches need to use styles and techniques *that are appropriate to the situation in which the learner is operating*. The appropriate style and technique need to be employed with the right balance of personal coaching skills. The most important of these are, probably, listening, questioning and giving feedback. We shall be looking at these skills in more detail later.

Opportunities for coaching arise on many different occasions during the working day, and it is important to seize them when they occur. This leads some people to argue that there is little need for formal planning, and that the best coaching is informal and relies almost entirely on questioning and immediate feedback.

My own experience suggests, however, that creating awareness and a sense of personal responsibility requires time for proper planning if genuine development is to be achieved. The two approaches are in fact complementary: although formal awareness and planning are important, informal coaching should take place wherever the opportunity arises.

Stage 4: evaluating for success

Many coaches confuse monitoring with evaluating. Monitoring is the essential activity of regularly checking that progress is being made in implementing the PDP. Evaluating is the activity of reviewing the PDP once it has been completed. It is a one-off activity involving the coach and the learner.

The key questions are:

- Were the developmental goals achieved?

- Did the different components of the PDP work in the sequences they were designed to?

- What changes, if any, were made to the PDP, and why?

- Was the PDP cost-effective?

- Were there any unexpected benefits?

- What would you do differently next time?

- Is there a need for a new PDP to improve performance still further?

It is clear that if the answer to the final question is yes (which it probably will be, because performance needs to improve continuously), then the whole coaching process needs to start again.

The importance of style

Being human, we find it quite tempting to think that what works well for us as a learning experience will also work well for others. There is often a strong tendency to impose our preferences on others. But research and experience show that there is considerable potential for conflict between different styles of working and learning.

A coach who has an 'activist' style, for example, is likely to get impatient with people who have a 'reflector or theorist' style, because they may not respond promptly to the spontaneous, unstructured, 'have a go' approach that appeals to the 'activist'. The same applies from a different perspective, because a 'reflector or theorist' coach's preference for a carefully planned, systematic and evenly paced approach will probably frustrate someone with a strong 'activist' style.

Learning to recognise and adjust to different styles is an important skill that coaches should develop. People's individual styles are not, of course, confined simply to learning preferences. Because style analysis is based on differences in temperaments and personalities, it also is a good guide to the way people prefer to work as well.

Coaching styles

In the same way that there are various learning or working styles, so there is a variety of coaching styles. But these are not based on a psychological analysis of the coach. Coaching styles are based on a continuum that ranges from situations in which the learner is completely inexperienced to situations in which the learner is highly experienced and capable.

The appropriate coaching style for inexperienced learners is termed the 'hands-on' style; for highly experienced learners, it is the 'hands-off' style. In between the two extremes is a variety of styles that the coach needs to be able to adopt, *depending entirely on the level of experience and performance of the learner.*

With someone who is completely new to a situation or who needs to develop a specific new skill, it may be entirely appropriate for a coach to adopt a 'hands-on', almost instructor-like, style. When dealing with an experienced high-performer, like an Olympic athlete or chief executive, it is more appropriate to adopt a 'hands-off' style and rely mainly on questioning and feedback skills.

Experience shows that the more rapidly a coach can move from a 'hands-on' to a 'hands-off' style, the faster improvement in performance will be achieved. The simple explanation for this is that as you move along the continuum towards 'hands-off', the more control and responsibility are transferred from the coach to the learner.

Coaching Olympic performers to reach even higher standards is a very sophisticated activity. The coach, who is often not at the same performance level as the performer, has to recognise that the performer has total control over performance. The Olympic coach operates in a 'hands-off' style and focuses largely on the mental attitude of the performer, rather than his or her basic skills and techniques. Coaches of top-performing teams and of stars in the performing arts have to follow this pattern too. The same approach is successful in the workplace. This transfer of control is illustrated in the following diagram.

Coaching management styles continuum

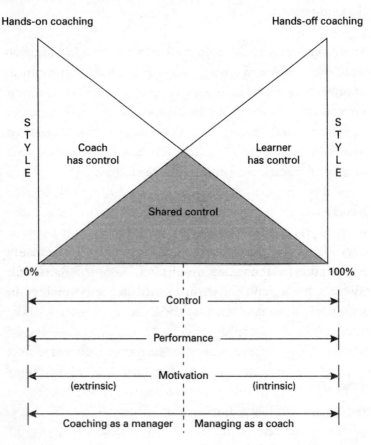

Managing as a coach

Many managers find it difficult to move quickly along the coaching styles continuum towards a 'hands-off' position. Partly this is because some managers are locked into a traditional hierarchical command-and-control management style and are ill-suited to and personally uncomfortable with changing style.

Sometimes, too, the culture of their organisation and job structure forces them towards a 'hands-on' style. For instance, in the case of a simple, repetitive task-oriented department with a high turnover of staff or a heavy reliance on temporary or short-contract people, a coach may be constantly forced into situations where 'hands-on' is the only appropriate style to adopt. Similarly, in situations of great urgency – such as a fire alarm – there is no time for a period of reflective questioning!

It is also true that where managers are held closely accountable for immediate results with severe penalties for failure, it is difficult for them to take the risk involved in letting go of control and trusting the performer to take responsibility for improving performance. This is a very real problem for many managers and has been made worse with the increases in workload and stress that have resulted from many experiments with re-engineering, the impact of new technology and mergers.

These pressures help to explain why many coaches and learners are probably operating at around 25–30 per cent of the way along the continuum towards a 'hands-off' style. There has been a lot of talk about sharing control and empowerment, but often there is a real, and understandable, reluctance to put it into practice.

There is of course a fundamental contradiction in this reluctance to change style. Experience shows that higher levels of performance from individuals and teams are more often achieved when people are given greater control and responsibility. So the desire and pressure for ever-higher performance standards are, in practice, frequently frustrated by a reluctance to risk releasing control. This frustration is likely to contribute to increased stress-levels for managers.

For organisations wishing to develop the necessary 'positive learning culture', there is no alternative but for managers to move rapidly down the coaching-style continuum towards the 'hands-off' position. This implies a change in management style away from 'coaching as a manager' towards 'managing as a coach'.

Coaching techniques

Among the most common situations that a coach can face are:

● coaching an inexperienced learner or helping to develop a new skill

■ finding time to help someone to sort out a problem when the coach is under the pressure of a heavy workload

▲ coaching an experienced and able learner who has the time and motivation to improve performance.

For each of these situations different coaching techniques can be employed. We shall look at each of them in turn.

Coaching inexperienced learners

The more inexperienced the learner is, the more 'hands-on' the coaching style will need to be. With complete beginners, the coach may well have to adopt the style almost of an instructor. One technique that has been found most helpful in these situations is called the 'practice spiral'.

The practice spiral starts with an initial explanation and demonstration stage. This is followed by a stage for reflecting on the learning achieved during the initial stage. Then comes a reviewing stage, which focuses on drawing specific conclusions about how much progress has been made towards achieving the eventual goal. The final stage involves planning to practise again. This of course leads to another new experience, but this time at a slightly higher level of performance.

The whole process begins again and continues to spiral towards higher and higher levels of performance after each new practice session. The process is shown in the illustration on page 20.

The 'practice spiral' technique

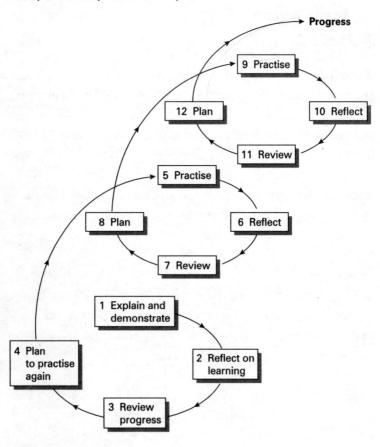

There are a number of key points for the coach to follow at each stage of the spiral.

Stage 1: explain and demonstrate
At this stage the coach should:

- summarise what is about to be explained and demonstrated

- emphasise why it is important

- outline how it is going to be done

- explain and demonstrate, following a logical sequence

- summarise, re-emphasising why it is important

- allow time for questions, clarifications and feedback to check understanding.

Stage 2: reflect on the learning

This stage should be deliberately timed. Often simply allowing a few minutes' private thought, note-taking or handling of a piece of new equipment is all that is required.

Stage 3: reviewing progress

At this stage the coach should remind the learner of the ultimate goal of the learning programme and encourage the learner to articulate the progress he or she believes to have made so far. Skilful questioning can help learners identify any barriers to learning they are experiencing as well as enabling them to clarify any areas of misunderstanding that may have arisen.

Stage 4: planning to practise again

Opportunities to practise what has been learned are crucial to ensure that the required competence standards are achieved. The coach should ensure three types of practice session:

- ● 'risk-free' opportunities, where mistakes can easily be made and remedial action taken with no damage done or blame expressed

- ■ 'close-observation' opportunities, where learners can practise real-life situations, with the coach in close attendance to be able to help correct any faults and to build confidence with constructive feedback and praise

- ▲ 'spot-check' opportunities, where the learner is free to operate in a real-life situation but with the knowledge that there will be occasional spot-checks by the coach to offer feedback and motivation.

As learners progress up the spiral the type of practice session the coach will agree with the learner will obviously move from 'risk-free' to 'spot-check'. Note that although the spiral starts with a totally 'hands-on' style, the coach moves steadily down the styles continuum towards a 'hands-off' position.

Remember, the spiral is a theoretical model and does not have to be slavishly copied. The context in which you are working will determine how the model should be varied to work effectively for your learner.

The '3-D' technique

Sometimes people ask for help at inconvenient times for the coach. Most managers are under increasing time-pressures and may genuinely find it difficult to reorganise their priorities to meet the immediate needs of a member of their team. Experience has shown that coaches who can cope with these situations are highly regarded by their colleagues and team members. Successful coaches often express the belief that time spent in coaching to help with immediate problems is repaid many times over through the improvements in performance and higher levels of motivation.

The essence of handling these pressurised coaching sessions is to focus as rapidly as possible on potential solutions that the other person can recognise and take personal responsibility for implementing. The '3-D' technique is one that has been found helpful for these situations. It is based on recognising a three-dimensional (3-D) analysis, as illustrated on page 24.

To use this technique, a coach needs simply a blank sheet of paper or a flip chart. The learner is asked to quickly define the problem in a single sentence. Careful questioning and using the 3-D analysis technique enable the coach and the learner to quickly identify three elements of the problem under each of three headings:

- *the situation* eg time-scales, lack of resources, geography

- *people involved* eg unhappy customer, impatient boss, unreliable supplier

- *you* eg lack of technical knowledge, conflicting priorities, your general attitude.

The '3-D' technique

```
                    ┌─────────────────────┐
                    │      PROBLEM        │
                    └─────────────────────┘
                              ↓
          ┌───────────────────────────────────────┐
          │  Single-sentence definition of problem │
          └───────────────────────────────────────┘
                              ↓
```

HURDLES

Brainstorm to establsh three aspects of problem relating to:

1   the situation   _____
    _____
    _____

2   people involved   _____
    _____
    _____

3   you   _____
    _____
    _____

OPTIONS

Select one priority issue from each aspect:

1 _____

2 _____

3 _____

APPROPRIATE ACTION

Choose one or more options to make progress:

1 _____

2 _____

3 _____

With these three dimensions or aspects of the problem identified, it is usually relatively easy to identify several options to choose from – even if most of them require actions related solely to the learner him- or herself!

The final stage is to choose the 'best-fit' option to implement.

Following this structured technique it is possible to focus rapidly on potential actions. By relying almost entirely on questioning, the coach can help people to articulate most of the issues and options themselves. The coach will have enabled the learner to focus more clearly and leave the responsibility for taking final decisions with him or her. With practice, this technique can work in 10–15 minutes.

It is also possible to use the 3-D technique to coach yourself through a problem. You can try it for yourself now:

1   Define a current problem in a single sentence.

2   List three general issues relating to the problem *situation*.

3   List three issues relating to the *people* involved.

4   List three issues that relate specifically to *you* and the problem.

5   Choose one issue from each of your three lists of three issues.

6   Now identify one or more options that are most likely to make progress in solving the problem.

It may seem rather simple, but it works. The technique works best when the coach relies entirely on questioning to encourage the learner to work through the process.

The GROW technique

The GROW technique has its origins in sports coaches who have been influenced by Tim Gallwey's book *The Inner Game of Tennis*. The technique relies heavily on using skilful questions and following a clear structure.

First, the questions focus on the GOAL that the learners want to achieve in the immediate coaching session. Next, the focus is on the total REALITY in which the learners are operating. This is followed by questioning the practical OPTIONS that the learners might choose to achieve the goal that they have set themselves. Finally, the focus is on the WILL to actually take specific action to implement one or more of the options previously chosen.

So the easy way to remember the structure is to use the mnemonic that summarises the GROW technique as:

- establish the **G**oal
- check the **R**eality
- consider all **O**ptions
- confirm the **W**ill to act.

GROW is a powerful technique when you are coaching learners who already have a basic knowledge, expertise and enthusiasm for the issue involved. This is generally true in a sports context but is often not the case in work situations. With inexperienced learners – or coaches, for that matter – the GROW technique is, in my experience, too time-consuming and sophisticated for practical, day-to-day, work-based coaching.

However, where the coach has the time, patience and skills the GROW technique is excellent for the 'hands-off' coaching style, with a proven record of success. The key skills are effective questioning and systematic following of the GROW structure during the coaching session. It is often an interactive process and cannot easily be rushed. The result of coaching with GROW can be a highly focused and motivated learner.

Coaching for successful team performance

A team can be defined as 'two or more people working together to achieve results'. In practice, a coach can usually expect to be effective with teams of about 12 to 15 people. Beyond that size more than one coach is often required.

The effectiveness of a team is the sum of the individual members' contributions. Tim Gallwey is credited with articulating the formula:

POTENTIAL minus INTERFERENCE equals PERFORMANCE

This positions the coach's main task as reducing or removing the 'interferences' that block an individual or team from producing their optimum levels of performance. The coach therefore has to harmonise individual effort into cohesive team action in order to achieve the desired performance results. The basic rules of coaching as a process requiring the application of styles, techniques and skills also apply to team-coaching. But, in addition, a team coach needs to understand the fundamentals of team dynamics and the different ways that individuals can contribute to successful team performance.

Comparing successful sporting teams to the world of work can be useful. The foundations of successful sporting teams are built on the coach's ensuring:

- that there is the right number of players with the basic skills, experience and knowledge of the rules of the game

- good matching of players to positions, and players who know what is expected of them individually and as a team

- regular training and practice on good, well-maintained equipment

- good communication of strategy and tactics

- regular reviews on performance, with encouraging and supportive feedback

- that mistakes are treated as learning opportunities and not occasions for blame and punishment.

This combination of technical expertise and the development opportunities and attitudes is equally true of work as of play.

Helicopter v seagulls

Team-coaching requires the coach to operate in one-to-one situations as well as in small and large groups. The GROW technique has proved successful in providing a structure to handle this wide variety of situations, although the coach should develop a special expertise to handle a group discussion using the GROW technique.

A successful team coach also needs to develop a 'helicopter' quality. This is the ability to rise above day-to-day events and pressures and take an overview of what is actually happening or likely to happen. It is rather like hovering in an aerial position so that 'the wood can be seen from the trees'.

Taking this more detached and objective view not only allows the coach to swoop down to help correct individual problems but also quietly to resume a more detached strategic and tactical view, allowing the team maximum control of its immediate performance.

The 'helicopter' quality is quite different from a 'seagull' quality. A 'seagull' coach is best described as someone who flies in, circles around, makes a lot of noise, swoops down and craps on a few people before quickly flying off again!

Assessing your coaching competence

To assist yourself in summarising the messages of this chapter, you may care to complete the following self-assessment exercise, which will help to establish your current levels of competence as a coach. Our own perceptions are often more critical than others'. But we may also be unaware of some aspects of our behaviour. Self-assessment is a powerful technique for raising awareness and providing an agenda for open dialogue with your colleagues and your coach.

Assessing your coaching competence

PERFORMANCE CRITERIA

Assessment Guidelines

There are three commonsense levels of assessment:

Good	which is above standard
OK	which is acceptable
Needs help	which is self-explanatory and is the information on which to base a PDP

1 Analyse for Awareness

You accurately assess the current standards of performance of the learner as an individual and as a team player.	☐ Good ☐ OK ☐ Needs help
You accurately identify the future performance goals of the learner, and gain positive agreement to attain them.	☐ Good ☐ OK ☐ Needs help

You analyse the learner's preferred learning style and identify any barriers to learning.

- ❑ Good
- ❑ OK
- ❑ Needs help

The techniques you use encourage the learner to develop an all-round awareness of themselves and their working environment.

- ❑ Good
- ❑ OK
- ❑ Needs help

2 Plan for Responsibility

You agree learning opportunities most suited to the learning style preferences of the learner.

- ❑ Good
- ❑ OK
- ❑ Needs help

Your skills coaching plan is based on the correct sequence of the components of the skill.

- ❑ Good
- ❑ OK
- ❑ Needs help

You agree methods of regularly monitoring performance and choosing opportunities for applying the learning.

- ❑ Good
- ❑ OK
- ❑ Needs help

You maximise the scope for the learner to manage their own development and take responsibility for meeting their goals.

- ❑ Good
- ❑ OK
- ❑ Needs help

You organise the appropriate time and space for the learner to practise skills and gain experience in a structured way.

- ❑ Good
- ❑ OK
- ❑ Needs help

You agree and/or facilitate the appropriate level of support for the learner.

- ❑ Good
- ❑ OK
- ❑ Needs help

PERFORMANCE CRITERIA

3 Implement for Action

You adjust your coaching style and technique to take account of the learner's progress and level of performance.	❏ Good ❏ OK ❏ Needs help
You explain and demonstrate skills and techniques using an appropriate manner and pace.	❏ Good ❏ OK ❏ Needs help
You ensure sufficient opportunities for practice, feedback and discussion to occur.	❏ Good ❏ OK ❏ Needs help
You ensure that adequate communication occurs with other people involved in the development process.	❏ Good ❏ OK ❏ Needs help

4 Evaluate for Success

You regularly evaluate the achievement of goals and standards and explore any factors inhibiting the learning.	❏ Good ❏ OK ❏ Needs help
You provide encouragement and support to the learner to apply their learning.	❏ Good ❏ OK ❏ Needs help
You motivate the learner to set new development goals and agree the ongoing support they need.	❏ Good ❏ OK ❏ Needs help

2 mentoring: similar but different

As with coaching, there are almost as many definitions of mentoring as there are individual coaches, mentors or tutors. The terms are often used interchangeably; however, the following three definitions give an indication of the wide variety of interpretations of mentoring in the workplace:

Mentoring is an essential aid to staff development...which calls for a perspective that looks for future possibilities. This requires a level of trust missing from the judgemental line management relationship where discipline has to be maintained and performance assessed.

David Megginson, Sheffield Business School

Mentoring includes coaching, facilitating, counselling and networking. It is not necessary to dazzle the protégé with knowledge and experience. The mentor just has to provide encouragement by sharing his enthusiasm for his job. ·

David Clutterbuck, Everyone Needs a Mentor

Good mentors are:

● good motivators, perceptive, able to support the objectives of the programme and fulfil their responsibilities to the candidate

■ high performers, secure in their own position within the organisation and unlikely to feel threatened by, or resentful of, the candidate's opportunities

▲ *able to show that a responsibility for mentoring is part of their own job description*

● *able to establish a good and professional relationship, be sympathetic, accessible and knowledgeable about the candidate's area of interest*

◉ *sufficiently senior to be in touch with the corporate structure, sharing the company's values and able to give the candidate access to resources and information*

● *good teachers, able to advise and instruct without interfering, allowing candidates to explore and pursue ideas even though they may not be optimum pathways*

■ *good negotiators, willing and able to plan alongside their own management teams and academics.*

Report of Council for
National Academic Awards and Government Training Agency

My research over recent years into mentoring as a management activity in the UK suggests that the word 'mentor' has become increasingly familiar, and typically describes various roles and responsibilities, which tend to fall into three distinct categories. These are:

● the 'mainstream mentor' acting as a guide, adviser and counsellor at various stages in someone's career, from induction through formal development to a senior management position

■ the 'professional qualification mentor' required by a

professional association to be appointed to guide a student through a programme of study leading to a professional qualification

▲ the 'vocational qualification mentor' appointed to guide a candidate through a programme of development and the accumulation and presentation of evidence to prove competence to a standard required for a National Vocational Qualification (NVQ).

Examples of these three roles can be found in many organisations – sometimes all three in a single, large organisation.

Mainstream mentoring roles are often designed to support specific groups:

● new recruits

■ graduate trainees

▲ women

● ethnic minorities

● disabled or disadvantaged individuals

● individuals facing a career change, redundancy or pre-retirement

■ people with a specific desire and motivation to manage their own learning and development.

Clearly, the term 'mentoring' is used to describe a wide variety of workplace activities. But lazy use of words that allows them to mean different things to different people within the same organisation is at best confusing and at worst dangerous. The need for clarity is imperative within organisations and should be the first task in any exercise to introduce mentoring. I suggest that the following definition makes a clear distinction between 'coaching' and 'mentoring':

The distinction between coaching and mentoring is one of roles, responsibilities and relationships.

A mentor is rarely a learner's line manager. Mentors will therefore be able to develop a special relationship as a friend and trusted adviser. They can be more interested in improvements in performance over a longer time-scale, possibly a whole career, than is the case with the necessary 'immediate results focus' of a line-manager coach.

Mentoring is also usefully seen as a process which supports learning and development.

This definition aims to make a distinction between coaching and mentoring for organisations with a typical line-management structure. In small organisations these distinctions may not easily apply. In some creative businesses with no real line-management structure, coaching may be defined as a responsibility for everyone in the organisation. In these cases mentoring may then be an additional role for only the top-management team with the responsibility to encourage, support and agree an individual's PDP.

But remember the caveat that 'workplace mentoring is always defined specifically by the context of the employing organisation'. Think for a moment of the different contexts between, say, a hard-driving, results-oriented financial services sales department and the essentially caring culture within which a healthcare professional operates. Mentoring is likely to have a different 'flavour', at least, in either context.

Mentoring as a process

Mentoring, like coaching, is a process. But whereas coaching is an enabling and helping process, mentoring is essentially a *supportive* process. The words used to describe each stage of the process reflect this distinction. The key stages in the mentoring process are:

● confirm the PDP

■ encourage self-management of learning

▲ provide support during the PDP process

◉ assist in the evaluation of success.

The use of these words also reflects the different roles and responsibilities of a mentor from that of a coach. In the workplace, mentors are rarely a learner's direct line manager, whereas a coach usually is. The mentoring process can be illustrated graphically as follows:

The mentoring process

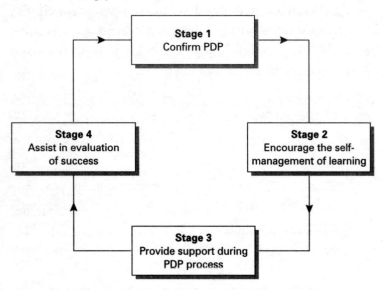

Let's now focus on some of the key tasks of a mentor during each stage of the process.

Stage 1: confirm the PDP

● Final responsibility for the PDP lies with the learner and his or her 'manager coach'. A mentor may be involved at any stage during the preparation of the PDP, but his or her role is simply to help confirm by providing guidance, access to information and acting as a 'sounding-board'.

■ The mentor has to prepare for this role by analysing, identifying and anticipating the likely needs the learner will have in achieving learning and developmental goals. The mentor will need to be sensitive to all the circumstances within which the learner is operating, including personal beliefs, capabilities, aspirations and learning-style preferences.

▲ The mentor needs to encourage the development of self-awareness in the learner by showing how self-assessment, and honest open questioning, can help achieve this.

● One of the key areas where a mentor may help is by checking that all the learning and developmental goals meet the SMART criteria (ie that they are Specific, Measurable, Achievable, Relevant and Timed – see page 61).

Stage 2: encourage the self-management of learning

● One characteristic of a good PDP is the extent to which it allows for self-management of the process. But not all learners will have sufficient experience to manage the implementation of the PDP. The mentor's greater experience should allow him or her, by asking probing questions, to encourage the learner to think ahead and anticipate some of the administrative aspects of implementing the PDP.

■ The mentor can also provide a useful service by giving clear explanations and reminders at the appropriate moment of the range of support options that may be available.

▲ One of the most critical aspects of the mentoring role is to ensure that the day-to-day working relationship between the learner and the line manager is not compromised by the mentor's activities. Learners should be encouraged on all occasions to work out their own solutions to any problem they have with their line manager or other colleagues. A mentor is a 'sounding-board', not a trouble-shooter. Conversations need to be in strict confidence so that a genuine level of trust can exist. Only in the most extreme situations should a mentor intervene directly. Adopting a genuinely objective, confidential and impartial role may not always be easy in practice, but it is essential.

Stage 3: provide support during the PDP implementation process

● As soon as the PDP starts to be implemented, the mentor needs to be available to provide support. In practical terms this means agreeing a schedule of meetings as frequently as seems necessary. It is also useful to agree methods for arranging impromptu meetings or contact to deal with any urgent and unforeseen difficulties.

▨ The style in which the mentor provides guidance and information is critical. Timing, pace and level are obviously important. But the danger of imposing the mentor's natural preferences must be guarded against. Avoiding bias of all kinds and remaining objective but at the same time staying fully involved is not always an easy balance to strike.

▲ Mentors will sometimes be asked to provide advice and make suggestions. The key here is to ensure that advice and suggestions are given only when requested and not imposed on the learner in an attempt to appear helpful. The mentor is definitely not expected to be the source of all knowledge and information, and should be quite willing to direct learners to alternative, and perhaps more appropriate, sources.

● A key role for the mentor is to help learners deal with mistakes and setbacks which, in some line-management relationships, may result in blame, guilt and feelings of inadequacy. The mentoring relationship should be non-judgemental and 'risk-free'. This allows the mentor to help the learner to treat mistakes and setbacks as real learning opportunities. Properly handled, these situations are often rich learning experiences.

● At all times, the mentor should try to build self-confidence and motivation in the learner in order to develop a positive attitude and a will to complete the PDP.

Stage 4: assist in the evaluation of success

● There is a distinction between regular monitoring of progress and final evaluation at the end of the PDP. A mentor's role is to encourage learners to arrange formal evaluations with their line managers.

■ Helping the learner to prepare for a formal evaluation is a useful mentoring function. Reminding them of the value of self- and peer-assessment of performance standards is particularly helpful.

▲ Mentors can use reflective questions to help learners analyse the causes of any barriers to learning that occur, as well as quantifying the benefits that were gained by themselves and the organisation during the PDP process.

● Formal mentoring relationships must at some time come to an end. Most often this occurs when a learner changes job or when a professional or vocational qualification is achieved. Ending a relationship is not always easy. Celebrating success and recognising the mutual benefits gained are important. The mentor should make a special effort to encourage the learner to continue to set new developmental and career goals. Agreeing to maintain interest and contact in the future is a positive note to end on.

Choosing mentors

Research and experience suggest that many people choose their own mentors to help them cope with the pressures of work and career development. Sometimes these mentors are partners, friends or professional colleagues in other organisations. It can be argued that it is more important for people to feel they have access to a mentor chosen voluntarily rather than have one formally appointed. But many organisations do not have this option and see value in formalising mentoring relationships.

I have emphasised the importance of clarifying mentoring roles, responsibilities and relationships. Everyone's expectations about the nature of the mentoring role should at least start from the same position. But some human resource professionals exaggerate the difficulties involved in selecting and pairing. In my opinion, they tend to translate the issues of mentoring in non-work situations with disadvantaged, disabled or partly dysfunctional children and adults into the more robust environment of the workplace. I have never heard of someone's problems being made worse by a mentor simply asking 'Tell me about it.' Acting as a sounding-board is a skill that most people possess. There is a potential danger, however, if the mentor chooses to respond by starting to give advice, because that is not the role of the work-place mentor. When the mentor senses a situation beyond his or her experience and capabilities, it is better to steer the learner towards a more expert source of help and advice.

Nevertheless, care needs to be taken before someone is appointed as a mentor or accepted as a volunteer for such a role. The normal criteria or working assumptions in most mentoring schemes are that mentors should be:

● older than the learner

■ already qualified or more knowledgeable

▲ more experienced in the job or longer serving in the organisation

- willing and able to do the job.

To help decide whether you (or someone else in your organisation) would meet that last criterion, you may care to complete the self-assessment opposite.

If you have given 10 'Definitely' answers, you are an ideal candidate to become a mentor and should volunteer at once. If you have even two 'Not at all' answers you should seriously reconsider your willingness to become a mentor. Most people will probably be somewhere between these two extremes. After careful discussion, and with a genuine willingness on your part to develop in any areas of perceived weakness, you should be able to take on a mentoring role with some confidence.

Mentoring techniques

All mentors would probably benefit from mastering each of the coaching techniques already discussed. In practice, mentors are likely to find the GROW technique (see page 26) applies most often in their role. This technique relies heavily on questioning skills, which is probably the skill the mentor needs to use most.

The essentially supportive nature of mentoring means that the issues of increasing motivation and building self-confidence are vitally important. All mentors would find it helpful to become familiar with motivation theories.

Mentoring volunteers' health-check

Tick the appropriate box under each question.

1   Do you understand how mentoring differs from other roles
    you are asked to play in your organisation?

    Definitely ❑   Partially ❑   Not at all ❑

2   Do you really want to take on the role, and are you willing to
    make the necessary time available?

    Definitely ❑   Partially ❑   Not at all ❑

3   Are you comfortable about being asked to assess your own
    strengths and weaknesses and relate them to the learner's
    developmental needs so that you can guide him or her to
    other sources of help, where it is appropriate?

    Definitely ❑   Partially ❑   Not at all ❑

4   Are you sure that you can invest time early on in the
    relationship to establish rapport and a regular schedule for
    discussions?

    Definitely ❑   Partially ❑   Not at all ❑

5   Do you know how to enable the learner to produce a
    realistic development plan and ensure that it is 'signed off'
    by all the relevant people?

    Definitely ❑   Partially ❑   Not at all ❑

6   Will you be able to keep the relationship on a professional level, particularly where there are differences in gender? (Sensitivity to potential misinterpretation in language and behaviour will be important in these situations.)

Definitely ❑   Partially ❑   Not at all ❑

7   Do you understand the distinction between counselling and advising, and whenever possible will you encourage the learner to work out their own solutions, yourself acting only as a sounding-board?

Definitely ❑   Partially ❑   Not at all ❑

8   Are you aware that you will be a role model, and that how you are seen to manage in day-to-day situations will affect the relationship you have with the learner?

Definitely ❑   Partially ❑   Not at all ❑

9   Are you sure that the feedback you give will be clear, honest and constructive, and designed to build confidence and ongoing commitment in the learner?

Definitely ❑   Partially ❑   Not at all ❑

10   Will you be able to recognise when the time has come to end the relationship, and aim to end on a positive and supportive note by sharing the value that both of you have gained from the experience?

Definitely ❑   Partially ❑   Not at all ❑

To help you reflect on many of the issues in this section and to gauge your current level of competence as a mentor, complete the following self-assessment check-list.

Assess your mentoring competences

PERFORMANCE CRITERIA

Assessment Guidelines

There are three common-sense levels of assessment:

Good	which is above standard
OK	which is acceptable
Needs help	which is self-explanatory and is the information on which to base a PDP

Stage 1: Confirm the Development Plan

You identify and agree specific needs for guidance.

❏ Good
❏ OK
❏ Needs help

You ensure that information and guidance given avoids bias and takes account of individual learning styles and the learning context.

❏ Good
❏ OK
❏ Needs help

You ensure that information and advice given covers choice of any relevant qualification process.

❏ Good
❏ OK
❏ Needs help

You encourage the use of self-assessment to develop self-awareness.

❏ Good
❏ OK
❏ Needs help

You confirm that any development goals are SMART.

❏ Good
❏ OK
❏ Needs help

Stage 2: Encourage Self-Management of Learning

You help to identify the range of factors that need to be managed to achieve learning goals, including the competences and resources required.

❏ Good
❏ OK
❏ Needs help

You help to identify the causes of any difficulties that arise and encourage learners to work out their own solutions.

❏ Good
❏ OK
❏ Needs help

You ensure that the relationship with the line manager is never compromised by any advice and guidance you offer.

❏ Good
❏ OK
❏ Needs help

You explain clearly the range of support available to manage the learners' own learning.

❏ Good
❏ OK
❏ Needs help

Stage 3: Provide Support during Development Plan

You agree a regular schedule of meetings and establish methods of gaining access to you as and when need for support arises.

❏ Good
❏ OK
❏ Needs help

You offer, but never impose, opinions and suggestions and, where appropriate, refer to other sources of guidance.

❏ Good
❏ OK
❏ Needs help

You ensure that guidance is given in a timely manner, at a level and pace appropriate and in such a way that it avoids bias.

❏ Good
❏ OK
❏ Needs help

You conduct and conclude discussions in a manner that promotes effective working relationships.

❏ Good
❏ OK
❏ Needs help

You encourage mistakes and setbacks to be seen as learning opportunities and build self-confidence and motivation to achieve goals.

❏ Good
❏ OK
❏ Needs help

Stage 4: Assist in the Evaluation of Success

You encourage formal evaluations of PDPs with line managers.

❏ Good
❏ OK
❏ Needs help

You ensure thorough preparation for formal evaluations by conducting assessments of the achievement of standards with peers and colleagues.

❏ Good
❏ OK
❏ Needs help

You help to identify any factors inhibiting the learning process as well as identifying any unexpected benefits gained during the learning experiences.

❏ Good
❏ OK
❏ Needs help

You offer encouragement and ongoing support to apply the learning.

❏ Good
❏ OK
❏ Needs help

You motivate individuals to set new development goals and help to identify any support they will need.	❏ Good ❏ OK ❏ Needs help
If appropriate, you ensure that the mentoring relationship ends on a constructive and positive note.	❏ Good ❏ OK ❏ Needs help

You have probably highlighted areas where you need to plan some personal development. Before you do so, why not check your self-assessment with a colleague – or *your* mentor? Often our own perceptions are more critical than those of others. But we may also be unaware of some aspects of our behaviour. Self-assessment is a powerful technique for raising awareness and providing an agenda for open dialogue.

essential skills and attributes

Listening, questioning and feedback are the most important skills to develop, and each of these is treated separately. I have also included the skills of goal-setting and development-planning, because these are skills with specific relevance to coaching and mentoring. Finally I discuss the attributes that help to turn the coach and mentor into a credible role model.

Listening and observing to assess performance

If you have ever participated in games or exercises where several people are shown the same picture and asked to describe what they see, you will know that the result is often contradictory interpretations. All kinds of obstacle impair visual communication – not just poor eyesight! People's expectations, assumptions, prejudices, wishes – all influence the messages received from observing and listening. Coaches and mentors rely heavily on these skills and need to be able to apply them effectively.

A coach using a 'hands-on' style needs, for instance, to listen to a learner's reply not only for accuracy but also for the note of confidence in the learner's voice. This confirms whether the coach's message has really been understood. Confidence, and other emotions, is expressed as much in the tone of the response as in the actual words themselves. A coach using a 'hands-off' style relies very heavily on questioning skills and has therefore to listen to and interpret the response, at the same time deciding very quickly on the next appropriate question. Pausing to reflect on the answer given is often a sensible technique. But having to ask for the answer to be repeated because of lazy listening damages the coach's credibility.

There are numerous books and training packages that cover in great depth the development of listening skills (see Chapter 6), but the following check-list covers the essentials:

1 Show you are interested by maintaining eye-contact and a friendly expression.

2 Be alert to the tone of voice being used. Sometimes it is more important how something is said (and done) than precisely what. This can be a two-way concern, so be alert to your own tone also.

3 Encourage the learner to describe ideas and opinions freely by using such prompts as 'Hmm', 'Yes', 'I see', 'So what happened then?'

4 Show the learner that you sympathise with his or her feelings – however they are expressed!

5 Don't take the learner's views personally, and try not to get defensive in response to any aggression.

6 Make a habit of keeping notes, because relying on your memory can be dangerous.

7 When dealing with complicated situations you should try to summarise your understanding by using such phrases as 'So what I think you're saying is...' or 'Let me play that back to you just to check...'.

8 Don't be too quick to come to conclusions or to start giving advice.

9 Don't argue or interrupt.

10 Remember the saying, 'God gave you two eyes to see and two ears to listen, but only one tongue so that you can see and hear twice as much as you can talk.'

Just to check you've taken these ideas in, perhaps you would care to read through the 10 tips again. Now ask yourself:

● Which of these tips do I already usually follow?

■ Which of these tips should I pay most attention to and try to apply more often?

▲ Which of these tips suggest areas that I may need help with to improve my skill level?

● Is there anyone I should contact to get a second opinion on the answers I have just given?

Questioning dos and don'ts to raise awareness

Developing questioning skills takes time, but we have already established how vital this is to successful coaching and mentoring. There are several well-known books and learning packages you can use to help point out the important distinctions between open and closed questioning or appropriate and inappropriate questions for different situations. However, the following lists of the 'dos and don'ts' of questioning should prove helpful.

Do

- be prepared to explain clearly why you need to ask questions

- work hard to build rapport and put the other person at ease by adopting a friendly, supportive and helpful manner

- try to ask clear, concise and specific questions

- always acknowledge answers positively and in an encouraging tone

- probe, when you need to, for extra information, and try using such phrases as 'Is that all?' or 'Are you sure we have covered everything?'

- give answers real consideration before responding – a pause will often show that you have done so

- realise the importance of developing self-awareness by using such questions as 'How did you feel as you did it?',

'When and where did you think your performance began to improve?' or 'Why do you think you got that response?'

Don't

- be afraid to use silence when appropriate; it may intimidate, so be careful, but it can provide additional, sensitive information because people often feel the need to keep talking if you keep quiet

- ask long-winded questions, because they will probably not be understood

- ask leading or loaded questions: they usually demonstrate only what you already know rather than what the learner or protégé really knows, thinks, or feels

- ask trick questions (unless you can explain the purpose), because they can cause resentment and be demotivating

- use complex, inappropriate language or jargon – you want to be understood, not create confusion

- assume you know the answer, or jump to the conclusion that what you hear first is the complete answer

- be side-tracked by answers that are interesting but not relevant to the issue you are dealing with.

Again, just as a check you may care to answer these questions:

● How many of these questioning dos and don'ts apply to you?

■ Think of the last time you had a coaching or mentoring session or conducted an interview or assessment. Do you think you broke any of the rules of questioning outline above? If the answer was yes, what could you do to avoid making the same mistakes again?

Feedback: the fuel that drives the motivation to learn and develop

Most experts agree that feedback skills are important in coaching and mentoring. Feedback can drive the motivation to continue to learn and develop in two directions. Get it wrong and motivation goes backwards fast. Get it right and motivation goes forwards steadily towards achieving the goal.

There are some basic barriers to both giving and receiving effective feedback:

● Feedback can come as a surprise or shock when there are no clear objectives for the job, or when the employee and manager do not share the same perception of what the job entails.

■ The feedback may be delivered in a way that the recipient sees as concentrating on critical or unsubstantiated judgements that offend the recipient's sense of fairness.

▲ There may be a problem of credibility: it is important

that the recipient believes the feedback-giver is competent to comment on those points.

● Previous history of receiving negative feedback may make the recipient feel obliged to 'defend his or her corner'.

● People are 'afraid' to give feedback because they are not confident about handling the response and are concerned that feedback will damage relationships.

Practical tips

There is a number of things you can do to make sure that you get a constructive response when you actively seek feedback:

● Identify who is best placed to provide you with feedback; this may vary depending on the circumstances each time and may involve more than one person. The concept of 360-degree feedback argues that you should seek feedback from all around you – managers, colleagues, suppliers and customers.

■ Choose a time and place appropriate to having a constructive discussion.

▲ Be clear about what you need feedback on, and don't try to cover too many things in one discussion – focus on the key issues only.

● Challenge the person giving you feedback if you feel he or she is not being completely honest or specific enough for the information to be useful to you.

● Ask probing questions to identify what behaviour you should continue doing or stop doing.

● Listen actively, concentrate and be receptive, because feedback is one of the most useful methods of learning.

■ Don't react defensively or try to justify poor performance that is being criticised, because learning from mistakes is a powerful opportunity.

▲ Spend some time reflecting on the feedback – don't reject it outright.

● Be aware that, although giving feedback is a difficult and unfamiliar process for some people, most will welcome the fact that you have sought their views and will be willing to help you to learn and develop.

● Always thank the person for giving feedback, to show that you respect the effort he or she has made, and indicate what you intend to do as a result.

Here is a check-list of some key dos and don'ts to follow when you are giving feedback – which, as a coach or mentor, you are likely to do very frequently.

Do
● remember that you get more out of people if you are sensitive to their situation and treat them as adults

- try to imagine how you would feel if you were on the receiving end

- make your feedback honest as well as fair, with a balance between both negative and positive messages

- be clear about weaknesses, but always try to emphasise strengths as well

- keep criticism simple and constructive by concentrating on behaviours, not personal attitudes or beliefs

- choose the appropriate time and place as well as the appropriate tone and language

- encourage people to take responsibility for their own development

- recognise that you will be taken as a role model, so practise what you preach.

Don't
- be quick to disagree or argue

- be overly critical

- be distant or aloof

- interrupt repeatedly

- ignore comments, ideas, feelings

- appear to be in a hurry to finish the session.

Finally, you should always remember that feedback fuels the motivation to learn how to improve performance. That is your main aim as a coach and mentor. So think carefully before you start to give feedback!

Once again, you may care to check your understanding by completing the following exercise. Think of two recent situations where, first, you received feedback on your own performance and, second, you gave feedback to someone else. Now provide answers regarding both situations:

- Was the feedback likely to help change future behaviour?

- Was there anything that could have been done differently to improve the quality of the feedback given?

- What was the most important thing you learned as a result of the feedback?

- Did you say thanks or ask for a response to your own feedback?

Agreeing development goals

You will recall that I have stressed the importance of setting clear developmental goals. But, unfortunately, in many situations goals are likely to be phrased in a rather general way – for example, 'To improve my ability to communicate and to present' or 'To present difficult ideas and problems in a way that aids understanding.'

A skilled 'manager, coach or mentor' should be able to help translate these woolly goals into developmental goals that are more focused. To do this, you may find it very helpful to apply the SMART technique. Goals are most useful when they are SMART, because it is much easier to prove whether they have been achieved or not. SMART provides a practical list of criteria that have to be met to ensure high-quality goals, as follows:

- **S**pecific (and Stretching)

- **M**easurable

- **A**greed (and Achievable)

- **R**ealistic (and Relevant)

- **T**imed.

Let's look at the criteria in a bit more detail. Each goal should be:

- **Specific** (and stretching) – related to a single desired result, and also understandable to those who will help you to achieve it. The goals should also be challenging and stretching to aim for levels of performance above present standards.

- **Measurable** – by containing a number of performance indicators. Quantitative performance indicators might specify dates, percentages or numbers to be achieved.

Qualitative performance indicators might quote or specify a standard required or refer to customer surveys or responses.

▲ **Agreed** (and achievable) – by checking that you can get the time, space and support you need to work on them; 'achievable', also, by using a defined process, such as good time-planning. This will also help you to set goals that are within your capability.

◉ **Realistic** (and relevant) – by being sensible about having the time available and about any other constraints in your work situation. Goals should always be relevant to personal and organisational objectives.

◉ **Timed** – to be achieved by a specified date. Work towards a goal should also be undertaken at the right time, ie when completion of the goal is technically possible.

The aim of all development is usually to bring about a change in the way people do things. This is why developmental goals should usually be written in behavioural terms. A developmental goal should state an intended outcome. It should describe what you will be able to do after completing the learning.

However, let me give one word of caution. In some cases 'development' might be interpreted as 'simply being made to feel valued'. The learner's 'goal' may be for the boss to change behaviour in a way that would help the learner to become more motivated and productive. When I was once faced with this very unusual situation, it reminded me forcibly that there are no absolutes, and that you have to be prepared to be flexible in your interpretations and work with the 'goals' as the learner chooses to express them.

Remember, though, that it is the coach (line manager) who has the responsibility for agreeing goals with a learner. The mentor's role is to help confirm that, as far as possible, the goal meets the SMART criteria. So both coaches and mentors need to understand the SMART technique. It is far more important, however, to be committed and self-disciplined enough to apply the technique in practice!

Agreeing a personal development plan (PDP)

SMART development goals are the main outcome of the 'analyse for awareness' stage of the coaching process. The next stage is to 'plan for responsibility', which requires an important skill to be developed.

Personal development plans (PDPs) are sometimes referred to as 'learning contracts'. The notion of 'contract' stems from the fact that these plans or contracts are verbally agreed between individuals and their 'manager coach'. In that sense, both parties have formally contracted with each other to meet the commitments laid down. Both have moral, if not strictly legal, obligations to fulfil the contract.

For the coach, who is very often the line manager, this can involve providing finance, resources, time and space. For the individual, it usually implies a high level of personal commitment to keeping to the schedule of review meetings and targets, as well as making available the necessary personal time. The mentor's role is to help confirm that the learner fully understands and accepts the implications in the plan by acting as a sounding-board or providing an objective second opinion.

In most organisations PDPs are quite simple in design. But they must contain the information essential to making them a useful document. Ideally the PDP should be reviewed at least once a month and should not cover more than three months; it otherwise tends to become a wish-list rather than a concrete plan.

The essentials are:

- What is the developmental goal, and is it SMART?

- How will the goal be achieved, and are all the main activities clearly listed?

- Where will the activities take place, and are there adequate facilities and resources available?

- When will the programme start and end, and how often will progress be measured and reviewed?

- Who is involved, and have they agreed to the plan?

One of the main obstacles to achieving a really useful PDP will be the generally negative attitude towards them. This has often been created by previous experience. In many situations the concept of the PDP has been fatally tarnished by association with the traditional 'annual appraisal scheme'. After the annual discussion and good intentions, the PDP has been all too often (I estimate in at least 70–80 per cent of situations) put in a drawer or filed away by the personnel department, never to see light of day until the following year's interview looms. Overcoming these types of attitude barrier should not be underestimated. The task is, however, to focus the learner on short time-scales and to reduce real achievements into bite-size chunks.

You may now care to complete the self-assessment on page 66 of your own current level of skills and personal attributes that an effective coach or mentor should ideally possess.

Assessing your current skills and attributes

PERFORMANCE CRITERIA

Assessment Guidelines

There are three commonsense levels of assessment:

Good	which is above standard
OK	which is acceptable
Needs help	which is self-explanatory and is the information on which to base a PDP

1 Skills

You establish rapport and open communication with learners.	☐ Good ☐ OK ☐ Needs help
You explain clearly any necessary concepts, information and techniques.	☐ Good ☐ OK ☐ Needs help
You give clarification, summaries and responses clearly, as required, and at the appropriate time.	☐ Good ☐ OK ☐ Needs help
You listen actively and positively.	☐ Good ☐ OK ☐ Needs help
You observe alertly and accurately.	☐ Good ☐ OK ☐ Needs help

Your questioning techniques are appropriate.

❏ Good
❏ OK
❏ Needs help

You display sensitivity and empathy to learners' thoughts and ideas.

❏ Good
❏ OK
❏ Needs help

You give feedback that is clear, concise, constructive and confidence-building.

❏ Good
❏ OK
❏ Needs help

You obtain acceptance and committment to performance goals from learners, and ensure that goals are SMART.

❏ Good
❏ OK
❏ Needs help

You encourage learners to accept responsibility for their own development by agreeing an appropriate PDP.

❏ Good
❏ OK
❏ Needs help

You recognise different preferred learning styles and adapt to them.

❏ Good
❏ OK
❏ Needs help

You actively help learners with special needs and difficulties.

❏ Good
❏ OK
❏ Needs help

2 Attributes

You show patience.

❏ Good
❏ OK
❏ Needs help

You have a sense of humour.	❏ Good ❏ OK ❏ Needs help
You avoid sarcasm and belittling people.	❏ Good ❏ OK ❏ Needs help
You are assertive, not aggressive or patronising.	❏ Good ❏ OK ❏ Needs help
You are firm but not domineering.	❏ Good ❏ OK ❏ Needs help
You are knowledgeable and skilful but willing to liaise with other experts as appropriate.	❏ Good ❏ OK ❏ Needs help
You demonstrate good time-management practices.	❏ Good ❏ OK ❏ Needs help
You are reflective and analytical.	❏ Good ❏ OK ❏ Needs help
You demonstrate confidence and self-belief.	❏ Good ❏ OK ❏ Needs help

You communicate a genuine belief in the potential for people to improve their performance.	❏ Good ❏ OK ❏ Needs help
You are able to manage emotions in yourself and others.	❏ Good ❏ OK ❏ Needs help
You act as a motivator and achiever both as an individual and as a team player.	❏ Good ❏ OK ❏ Needs help
You act as a good role model.	❏ Good ❏ OK ❏ Needs help

Assessing your skills and attributes

You may feel that you have to be something of a saint to meet these criteria. But don't be discouraged! Most people will be able to develop the necessary skills and attributes if they have sufficient determination. Given the importance of learning in the modern world of work, and given the important contribution that coaching and mentoring can make to supporting and enabling learning, the level of motivation to succeed should be high. I hope that completing these self-assessments will have helped. I also hope that they have been enjoyable, because this is a vital aspect of helping people to manage their own learning.

4 simplicity is the key

Reading the previous chapters may have created the impression that you need to be a combination of saint and superman before you contemplate becoming a workplace coach or mentor. Nothing could be further from the truth. I have been describing ideal models, best practice and highly desirable skills and attributes. But, to repeat myself, very few of us ever achieve 100 per cent perfection. The aim should be to do a good, competent and useful job in 'helping' (coaching) and 'supporting' (mentoring) learners to manage their own learning.

I have met very few people who cannot become good, competent and useful coaches and mentors. The key to success is not to overcomplicate the job or to erect unrealistic and unnecessary barriers and expectations. My golden rule in most things is that *success comes most surely from doing simple things consistently*. My six 'Rules of Simplicity' (below) reflect this approach to successful coaching and mentoring.

Simplicity rule 1: make sure you meet

By far the most common reason why coaching and mentoring schemes fail is that managers don't find the time to meet with their learners. Of course time-pressures are intense on all managers and, arguably, have become more so in recent years. But we all have the same time available to us. So the issue is really what we choose to do with it and what tools we can use to help us find the necessary 'extra' time.

The tool most commonly used to help to manage our time is, of course, the diary. I strongly advocate the use of some form of learning diary, in which both manager and learner commit to each other to meet on specific days each month. The simple act of both parties writing the commitment down increases the likelihood of its happening. But be honest. If you don't intend to keep the commitment, don't write it down.

Managers cannot preach the necessity for others to take personal responsibility for improving performance if they are not prepared to take personal responsibility for finding time to meet. It is as simple as that.

Simplicity rule 2: keep it brief

Time is precious, so there is no point wasting it. Formal coaching and mentoring sessions should be quite productive enough if they take between 30 and 75 minutes. If they are shorter, you don't really have time to become focused. But if sessions take longer they run a real danger of straying into becoming counselling or therapy sessions.

Not everyone will agree with this view. But remember the context I am writing about. The workplace is a robust environment and is possibly becoming even more demanding and unforgiving. I do not deny that counselling and therapy have an important role to play in the workplace. But I do believe that it is a job for specialists, and to expect all managers to be able to do it is unrealistic. On the other hand, I do believe that all managers can become good coaches and mentors.

I also acknowledge the need to be flexible in applying this rule. Sometimes situations are too stressful to be rushed. Sometimes learners need time to unburden themselves. Certain types of people simply don't respond easily to time-pressured situations. So the coach and mentor has to be willing to be both flexible and patient.

But this is where the 'make sure you meet' rule applies. Regular meetings allow the coach to vary the length of the meetings to take account of the occasional stressful or difficult session. But after, say, three of these necessarily lengthy sessions I would advise turning to another specialist for help. Coaches and mentors cannot be expected to be able to handle every situation, and they become potentially dangerous if they think they should.

Simplicity rule 3: stick to the basic process

At the most basic level, coaching and mentoring sessions are one-to-one meetings in which the learner chooses which issues to talk about and the coach and mentor listens and asks questions. But they need focus, structure and, especially, good time-management. Sticking to a simple process that ensures this happens is therefore crucial. So:

- Ask the learner either to come prepared with his or her agenda or spend the first few minutes agreeing it.

- Write it down and also manage the time spent on each item.

- Agree that taking notes is purely optional.

- Make certain, though, that you both write down any action point that the learner decides he or she genuinely wants to commit to do (and make sure it is Item 1 on the agenda for the next meeting).

- Agree the date and time for the next meeting.

The process really is as simple as that. If you stick to it you are signifying to the learner that:

- these are not management, operational or performance review meetings

- these are not appraisal meetings that require documentation for the personnel department

- these are not disciplinary meetings

- but these *are* meetings controlled by the learner and focused on the learner and his or her needs and ambitions. In mentoring sessions they are also meetings that are completely confidential.

Simplicity rule 4: develop the 'ask, don't tell' habit

Most managers quickly develop the habit of 'acting as managers are expected to act'. This varies from organisation to organisation depending on the prevailing culture (and probably on how many different training courses managers have attended!). It also depends on age, gender and personality type. But you can be pretty sure that there will be 'management-style habits'.

You can also be reasonably sure that many managers will be unfamiliar with acting as coaches and mentors and fully accepting the underlying philosophy that 'letting go of control = potential for higher performance'. The idea that good coaching and mentoring means moving quickly away from the 'hands-on' to the 'hands-off' position is one of the most difficult barriers for managers to jump.

But developing the 'ask, don't tell' habit is a vital new habit for managers to learn. Spelling it out as the '80 per cent asking questions and only 20 per cent giving answers' rule is another way I have found that helps some managers to adapt their style. But constant repetition and reminders of this rule are probably the best way to get it established.

Even managers who can accept this philosophy intellectually have real practical problems in applying it. Faced with the pressures of accountability for short-term results both in financial goals and customer satisfaction, many managers tend to revert to more traditional command-and-control techniques. To expect otherwise is unrealistic and unsympathetic.

Simplicity rule 5: remember, it's all about learning

Another real attitude barrier that busy managers have to jump is the concept of 'self-responsibility for learning'. Some people's deeply ingrained habit – and indeed preference – is to associate 'learning' with classroom or training course activities. Traditionally, organisations have taken primary responsibility for developing the skills and knowledge of their employees – and the responsibility, in many cases, for planning whole careers. The role of the line manager has largely been confined to conducting the annual appraisal and agreeing a 'wish-list' of training courses.

Coaching and mentoring sessions on a monthly basis, with discussions of a personal development agenda determined by the learner, represent a major change of behaviour for a large number of managers. In my experience only about 30 per cent of any management population will, in the short-term, be open to persuasion to try to implement this kind of change to their routines. Even then it will take three to four months before the benefits become apparent. But benefits there certainly will be, and patient persistence will be rewarded.

One of the benefits most likely to be noticed first (but resisted by professional trainers) is the real cost-effectiveness of coaching and mentoring compared with the results of simply sending people on courses away from the workplace. An hour of on-the-job learning and development that can be immediately related to current applications saves a great deal of time and money.

Persistently reminding managers that 'It's all about learning' and simply pointing out the real-life benefits helps to make coaching and mentoring become the habitual way 'we do things around here'.

Simplicity rule 6: expect to gain yourself

Benefits from coaching and mentoring are not a one-way street flowing only in the direction of the learner and organisation. Coaches and mentors almost always benefit equally by learning new techniques for getting results from the people they work with. There are also the less tangible benefits of the feedback from more highly motivated and appreciative colleagues.

Managers should not be embarrassed to acknowledge the 'self-interest' expectation. Indeed, I would positively encourage them to adopt this win-win attitude. Equally, it is worth emphasising that my definition of the overall purpose of coaching and mentoring includes 'helping people to become the person they want to be'. This opens up the possibility of rewards from outside the immediate environment of the organisational setting – and, without becoming too idealistic, also opens up the possibility of meeting moral and spiritual fulfilment.

5 developing the standards

The explosion of interest in coaching and mentoring over the last decade has transformed these activities from marginal to mainstream concerns in the management and development of people in the workplace. As previously quoted, 87 per cent of UK establishments now employ coaching and mentoring as part of their training and development programmes. Not surprisingly, there will be a growing debate about quality standards and best-practice methods. The debate will necessarily be wide-ranging to include the different situations in which coaching and mentoring are applied.

Once again there are no real absolutes. In the world of education and community action, for instance, there are quite well-established standards for helping and supporting people who need to learn how to deal with issues of disadvantage, diversity and disability. These are different again from the methodologies that are needed to work successfully with dysfunctional adults and children. In the world of work, too, coaches from a psychotherapy background advocate somewhat different standards and codes of practice from those of former sports coaches who have become popular business coaches. It is also regrettably true that a large number of training companies now label at least one of their interpersonal skills courses as 'coaching or mentoring'.

But there are broad trends that I shall discuss under the separate headings of 'professional bodies', 'academia' and 'occupational standards'. Finally, I will comment on the 'best' way to develop qualified coaches and mentors.

Professional bodies

Somewhere in the universal laws of creation is a force that decides that 'professional bodies and associations' will automatically come into existence as soon as a new area of intellectual study appears. These institutions serve a valid purpose for the exchange of information and research. They also appear to meet a human need to 'go to conferences', to 'read specialist magazines' and, most recently, to 'join discussion groups on the Internet'.

Mentoring has been no exception and I recommend you visit the following web-sites to find out more:

● **International Mentoring Association**, Western Michigan University at www.indianna.edu/-rugsdev/ima.html; or e-mail cedu_ima@wmich.edu; or tel. USA 616 387 4147

■ **European Mentoring Centre** at www.mentoringcentre.org; or e-mail emc@item.co.uk; or tel. 01628 661667

▲ **National Mentoring Network** at e-mail natment@aol.com

◍ **Mentors Forum** at www.mentors.forum.co.uk; or tel. 01727 813600

◉ **Mentors Network, Association for Management Education** at www.management.org.uk; or e-mail amed.office@management.org.uk; or tel. 020–7235 3505.

For those interested in developing contacts with the International Mentoring Association I have found the following people particularly responsive:

◉ Rey Carr in Canada at www.peer.ca/peer.html

■ Peg Boyle Single in the USA at pboyle@email.sjsu.edu

▲ Ann Ritchie in Australia at annritchie@yahoo.com

Academia

Coaching and mentoring have become legitimate areas of academic study and qualifications. Although mentoring may appear to be the main focus, coaching is often a significant part of study programmes. For those interested in finding out more, I would recommend you visit the following web-sites for more information on:

◉ PhD and masters programmes from the **University of Lancaster Business School** at www.lancs.ac.uk ; or tel. 01524 65201

■ a diploma in mentoring from **Leeds Metropolitan University** at www./mu.ac.uk/ces/ped/jowett,htm; or tel. 0113 283 2600 ext. 3971

▲ an undergraduate degree in human development and human communication are at least on the agenda at **Westminster College, Oxford** (currently merging with OxfordBrookes University) at e-mail d.langford@ox-west.ac.uk; or tel. 01865 247644.

Professional standards

There are broadly two approaches to professional standards. The first is the National Vocational Qualifications (NVQ) route and the other can be described as the 'business school' route.

The NVQ route has both its supporters and detractors. Government, and indeed European Social Fund, money is quite widely available to support the development of NVQ standards. Detractors focus mainly on the cost and clumsiness of assessment and the inappropriateness of this approach for the subject matter.

Most NVQ qualifications currently available are based on the occupational standards developed by either the Training and Development Lead Body (TDLB Units A21, A22, C21, C22, C25, C26, D11, E31) or the Management Charter Initiative (MCI Units C1, C2, C3, C9, C10, C11). Several of the Awarding Bodies offer qualifications based on different combinations of these standards, and for those interested in discovering more I would suggest you start at the **Institute of Personnel and Development** web-site at www.ipd.co.uk

It would also be useful to contact Ann Reynard and her colleagues at the **University of North London** at areynard@unl.ac.uk to ask for a copy of the standards that they have developed as a result of a project financed by the European Social Fund.

The first 'business school' qualification I would recommend you explore is **The School of Coaching**, which is a partnership between Myles Downey, the former tennis coach turned business guru, and the Industrial Society, the well-known training organisation. The School of Coaching targets high-flying executives and captains of industry. Their programme is based on an intensive series of taught workshops and practical coaching in the workplace. The masters-level qualification offered by the school is accredited by the University of Strathclyde. For more information I suggest you visit the Industrial Society's web-site at www.indusoc.co.uk, or tel. 020–8262 2401.

The Oxford School of Coaching and Mentoring is a 'virtual' business school. It provides qualified faculty as role-models to run internal workplace development programmes but does not offer taught courses or training programmes. The school offers qualifications at certificate, diploma and masters levels. More information can be found by visiting the web-site at www.oscm.co.uk, or tel. 01869 349192.

Is there a 'best way'?

There is definitely a growing consensus that coaching and mentoring qualifications are needed. Once established and accepted, they would provide a reasonable guarantee that a 'qualified' individual can deliver an acceptable level of service. They would also give organisations a quality standard of consistent and competent performance to expect from their managers. In the age of 'self-responsibility for future employability', obtaining a qualification is also a strong motivator for some people.

But there is no agreement on the 'best' way to develop or assess coaches and mentors for a qualification. This should not surprise anyone. The scope of the subject is huge. The contexts in which coaching and mentoring occur are infinitely variable and, to repeat myself, *it is the context that primarily determines what happens and what is needed.*

We also know that individuals have widely different preferences as to how they would choose to learn and develop. The wide variety of choice indicated in this chapter is therefore very healthy and, of course, there are many more opportunities available in addition to the ones mentioned.

So the search for a 'best' way is really a matter of opinion. I offer these questions for you to consider:

●   Why do we keep using training courses to develop coaches and mentors when we know that (charismatic trainers excepted) most training courses produce only limited impact on changes in behaviour in the workplace? (In the last century research by the German experimental psychologist Hermann Ebbinghaus produced results, validated since by scores of other researchers, that showed 90 per cent of what was learned in a class was forgotten within 30 days and 60 per cent was forgotten after one hour (the so-called 'forgetting curve').)

- If coaching and mentoring is such a good idea (remember the IPD survey that reported that over 50 per cent of trainers claimed it was more effective than training courses), why don't we use role-model coaches and mentors to develop other coaches and mentors?

- Should 'qualified' coaches and mentors have to produce results-focused evidence for assessment or, in other words, prove that they can deliver what they promise?

- Can coaches or mentors claim to be 'qualified' without producing evidence that they have a good grasp of theory and best-practice techniques or, put another way, that they know why they are doing what they are doing?

- Is a qualification essential for effective coaching and mentoring, or is feedback from the learner the only really important measure of success?

I immediately own up to the charge of asking exactly the type of leading questions that coaches and mentors should not use. So ignore them if you choose. Alternatively, suggest – and publish – other criteria we need to consider to help to establish standards of best practice, and so join in this important debate. There is a great deal still to learn and discuss. A good coach and mentor knows that 'every session, every event and every conversation is a two-way learning opportunity'. Good luck!

5 suggestions for further study

The following general reading list may be helpful.

ARGYRIS C. *On Organisational Learning*. Oxford, Blackwell, 1992.

BEE R. *and* F. *Constructive Feedback*. London, Institute of Personnel and Development, 1995.

BONE D. *A Practical Guide to Effective Listening*. London, Kogan Page, 1988.

BUCKLEY R. *and* CAPLE J. *One-to-One Training and Coaching Skills*. London, Kogan Page, 1991.

BUZAN T. *Use Your Head*. London, Ariel Books/BBC Books, 1984.

CLUTTERBUCK D. *Everyone Needs a Mentor*. 2nd edn. London, Institute of Personnel and Development, 1991.

DRYDEN N. *and* VOSS A. *The Learning Revolution*. Aylesbury, Accelerated Learning, 1994.

GALLWEY T. *The Inner Game of Tennis*. New York, Random House, 1974.

GOLDRATT E. M. *and* COX J. *The Goal*. Aldershot, Gower, 1989.

HEARSEY P and BLANCHARD K. *Situational Leadership*. University Associates, San Diego, California, 1982.

HEMERY D. *The Pursuit of Sporting Excellence*. London, Willow Books, 1986.

HONEY P. and MUMFORD A. *Using Your Learning Styles*. 2nd edn. Maidenhead, Peter Honey, 1983.

KALINAUCKAS P. and KING H. *Coaching: Realising the potential*. London, Institute of Personnel and Development, 1994.

LANDSBERG M. *The Tao of Coaching*. London, HarperCollins, 1996.

MACKAY I. *Asking Questions*. London, Institute of Personnel and Development, 1995.

MACKAY I. *Listening Skills*. London, Institute of Personnel and Development, 1995.

MAHESH V. S. *Thresholds of Motivation: The corporation as a nursery for human growth*. New Delhi, Tata, McGraw-Hill, 1993.

MAYO A. and LANK E. *The Power of Learning*. London, Institute of Personnel and Development, 1994.

MEGGINSON D. 'Less the teacher, more the friend'. *Works Management*, November 1996.

MORRIS D. *Manwatching: A field guide to human behaviour*. London, Cape, 1977.

MUMFORD A. *Effective Learning*. London, Institute of Personnel and Development, 1995.

PEASE A. *Body Language*. London, Sheldon Press, 1984.

SENGE P. *The Fifth Discipline*. London, Century Business, 1992.

TUTE W. 'Coming to terms'. *People Management*, April 1997.

WHITMORE J. *Coaching for Performance*. 2nd edn. London, Nicholas Brealey, 1996.

WHITMORE J. *The Winning Mind*. Hove, Fernhurst Books, 1987.